Dear Mama

If Only You Loved You

ISBN 978-0-578-38397-2 Paperback

ISBN 978-0-578-38482-5 E-Book

A special thank you to the women who have supported me along this journey, you mean the world to me.

Thank you Maurice Coleman for always being there, even when you didn't have to.

Instagram: Thomeisha

Email: Thomeishac@gmail.com

Table of Contents

Introduction

Dear Mama,

All of these years, I have felt so much anger and resentment towards you. I never thought there would come a day where I saw myself as anything like you. I never thought I would be able to forgive you for being so naive, gullible, and ignorant when it came to so many things in your life. One thing I knew for certain was that I would never forgive you for the pain, hatred, shame, and guilt that you instilled down on the inside of me at such a young age. Between the lack of our relationship, the abuse as a child, and watching your behaviors, I struggled to know my worth for so long.

What I didn't know was that the childhood trauma would have a rippling effect on me for the rest of my life. No matter how smart I was or how beautiful they said I was, I was insecure. Those insecurities led me to search for love in all of the wrong places. Places that would lead me to darkness. That darkness broke me. I got lost in the darkness. I would've done anything to get back into the light. That's when I realized I was just like you. Heroine was your escape from the darkness. The perfect temporary paradise away from all of the chaotic thoughts wrecking your mind. The only difference between you and me was that my drug was love.

Sometimes I wonder if only you loved you. If you loved you, then maybe you would have found another way through that darkness. If only you loved you, then you would have been able to love me. I wouldn't have spent every year until today searching for my drug in all of the wrong places. I imagine that you would have been able to warn me of all of the dangers that lie in the darkness of lust, how it could rip you to pieces with a few words or one wrong action. Then I realized that the same thing ripped you apart. If you were loved and weren't looking for it in the wrong places, you might not have ever found Heroine.

Truth is, Mama, I have never given you the credit you deserve for giving birth to my siblings and me and waking up every day to make something happen while we were in your presence. I can only imagine the pain you were feeling and how much you wanted to give up. I know you tried your best.

While neither of us owns a time machine or magical eraser to remove the pain you caused me growing up, I can tell you that it has turned me into a force to be reckoned with. You can feel better knowing that I finally know my worth. Every piece of trauma, every hardship, almost depleted me mentally, but I'm still here. I'm just like you, and you're just like me.

Chapter one
GROWING UP WITH YOU

I'm Thomeisha, your middle child, your baby girl. I'm the girl whose life has been tossed around from one bad hand to another. Life has taught me so many lessons before I could even choose which life I wanted for myself. For a long time, my life was chosen for me. The hardest lessons came from those who said, "I love you, Thomeisha." My confusion around love all started with you, Mama.

Growing up, the only mom I knew was Ma. I'm glad you left me with your mom because life wasn't all bad, from what I remember. I mean, we had to walk a couple of blocks to collect water to take baths and flush the toilet, but Ma was always there to give me a bath at night. We had to open the oven for heat to get into the house, but Ma was always there to hold me tight at night. Every Friday, she would give me twenty dollars to do whatever I wanted. The excitement I had just to walk to Family dollar to buy toys and twenty-five-cent cakes were priceless.

Ma only beat me once, I don't remember what I did, but it was a whipping I would never forget. My brother and sister won't either; they said she beat me so bad I was doing the percolator.

I think life was so good because I was able to just be an innocent child. There were no fears or worries, and if Ma had any problems, I never knew.

All of that changed in one night, though. You must know what night I'm talking about. It's a day that I don't remember too precisely, but it's permanently etched in my memory. I don't know where you came from. I don't know who those men were. I still don't know why they had those guns on me and my sister's heads. I used to wonder what they might've done if you and Ma didn't bring them that orange envelope. Would they have shot us all or just me and my siblings? Is that really how I would have lost my life? Would I really have just died at five years old for something that I had no idea about? Sitting on that porch was like being in one of those action movies we used to watch together. This was the first time I ever faced fear, anxiety, insecurity, defenselessness, helplessness, and danger. That wasn't the last time either, Mama, but I wish it was.

Life really changed for the worse when Ma lost the house. We all went to stay at the assisted living facility with some old man that Ma knew. There was only one room and one bathroom, of course. There was a tiny living room the size of a rich person's walk-in closet where me, my sister and my brother all slept on the couch or floor. Right next to that was a corner where the refrigerator, microwave, and front door were. It was right around the corner from our school Blackwell Elementary, so we still walked to school.

Honestly, the living arrangements weren't the worst part. Ma still made sure we ate, bathed, and she loved on us. The worst part was having to come live with you.

Initially, moving into the trailer park with you and Charlie wasn't so bad. Charlie was a white man who worked for the city, so he had enough money to provide for us. We had most of what we wanted. We got to play games on our Nintendo, we got to eat pizza and happy meals a lot, and I got to play solitaire on his computer. Even though we all shared a room, at least I only had to share a bed with my sister.

As a little girl, you know I loved chocolate so much. If I could have warped into Willy Wonka's Chocolate Factory, I would have. You used to say I was going to turn into chocolate. Every time Charlie went to the store, he was certain to buy chocolate cakes, ice cream, pudding and chocolate milk. He would let me sit on his lap and play Solitaire on the computer as long as I wanted to and eat as much chocolate pudding my stomach could take. I was in chocolate heaven. Looking back, I had everything I wanted. Let you tell it; I was spoiled rotten.

Then, one day, things became different. I was playing solitaire with Charlie like any normal heavenly day. A few minutes into the game, I felt something on my private parts. I froze because I didn't know what to do. I just sat there, stuck, still clicking the mouse, pretending to play the game. Charlie kept roughly pushing and rubbing his two fingers on my private parts. I felt like I should do something, but I didn't know what to do. I don't know what silenced me.

Did you know that he touched me when it first happened? Did you know that he was going to sexually abuse me? Did he tell you before he did it, or did he tell you after he did it?

I wasn't sure if I was supposed to say anything. I just knew that what he did was not supposed to happen to me. Immediately, it seemed like I was carrying the heaviest secret of my life. It reminded me of the time Ma gave me a bath and my private parts were bleeding. Ma asked me what happened, but I said nothing. Did Ma ever ask you what happened? Did you know what happened to me? Did you realize anything different about me like Ma did? Did the same thing happen to you when you were younger? Were you ever raped or molested? Is the reason Charlie moved out and left you with the trailer payments because you wouldn't allow him to touch me? There are so many unanswered questions raging in my mind. Now, I guess I have come to peace knowing that they may never be answered.

Times had gotten really rough. Your addiction was so bad. Heroin had such a strong hold over you. It seemed to be the only thing that mattered to you. If you didn't have it, you were so bitter and mean. One substance controlled your whole life. You became so fixated on having it that you were never around anymore. Chasing that high became your main priority. After all, it was euphoria for you. Four kids, a mountain of bills, and being surrounded by poverty would never give you that same feeling.

If your new boyfriend, AKA step daddy, wasn't there living with us paying the rent, we would've been homeless a lot sooner. Step daddy was mean, but he was nice to me. He didn't play about Aaliyah, my baby sister. I loved my baby sister. Aaliyah was so pretty, like a sweet little Gerber baby. She belonged on one of those food jars or in a magazine. Unfortunately, for five years, Aaliyah couldn't walk. I remember the doctors saying she would never walk or talk. It was such a miracle that we wanted to believe that one day she would talk too. I wonder what her life would be like today if she could talk. She would be smart if she didn't have cerebral palsy and epilepsy. Thank God that we were all in the car the night she had to be rushed to the hospital for a seizure. If not, we would have never known what to do for her that night when you never came home, and she had a seizure. I don't know which part was more terrifying: the fact that the four of us were home alone, her eyes rolling in the back of her head, or the foam running out of her mouth. Lucky for you, we kept her alive while you were only God knows where.

Step daddy must have gotten tired of your shit too. He stopped paying bills and stopped showing up for Aaliyah. His random disappearances turned into him never showing up again. I really knew it was getting bad when you were selling all of the food stamps, and we ate rice for breakfast, lunch, and dinner for like a week straight. So bad that we got evicted from the trailer park and had to go move in with Charlie again.

Why did he let us move there with him? It wasn't like he had the space for you and your four kids. I mean, it was a small two-bedroom house. I guess I would find out why later, though, huh?

We were having a pretty normal day; we got happy meals for dinner, which was my favorite. You and Charlie kept our drinks until a few minutes after we got home. I remember the fruit punch tasting like medicine, and I didn't want to drink it. We all complained about it but drank it anyway. Why would you put NyQuil in our drinks? Was that your idea or Charlie's?

Later that night, when everyone was asleep, you came whispering in my ear. Then you walked me to Charlie's room, where he was lying down without any pants or underwear.

Gosh, I hated Charlie's room. It always smelled like baby oil and cigarettes. He would always have a jar of vaseline and baby oil on his nightstand. Right next to it was an ashtray full of cigarette buds. There were inappropriate pictures of women who looked to me like prostitutes.

I felt so vulnerable and betrayed by you. You had said all I had to do was stand there and watch. Standing there was so agonizing and uncomfortable. That had to have been the worst and most disgusting thing that I have ever watched in my entire life. Once again, I was frozen in time. I didn't know what to think. Knowing that you were now a part of this, I didn't know who I could tell or talk to. Afterwards, Charlie gave you and me money, that's when I knew I wasn't supposed to say a word. You sold me out for Heroine Mama, really?

The next time you led me into Charlie's room, you said, "he just wants to kiss you." I was thinking, okay, give him a kiss, and Mama will have her money for drugs, and it will all be over. But then you told me to take my pants down. How could you stand there and watch him lick all over my private parts like that? It had to have been at least fifteen minutes, and you didn't even flinch. Was I really nothing to you? Wasn't I more important than your temporary euphoria?

Why couldn't my love be your drug? Why couldn't I be your motivation to want more for yourself and your children?

I'll never forget when it got to the point where you would make me go in there on my own. He would do whatever he wanted to do to me, but I guess in your defense, it would have been too hard for you to watch him penetrate me over and over, huh? I guess you had a few morals.

I can't believe you groomed me into being a rag for him. You really tried to teach me and make me comfortable. Was that really the life you wanted for me? I guess you couldn't see that far. You couldn't see how these experiences would be the catalyst of misery for the rest of my life.

Keeping the secret from my siblings was hard. I thought that they had to have known, heard something at night, or at least wondered where I would get cash from. It was even more challenging to go to school and act normal. I didn't fit in. I felt filthy and ashamed. I was shy, awkward, and relatively quiet, but I was smart. So smart that you never bothered to acknowledge my report card anymore. The only time I felt acknowledged by you was when it was time to go into Charlie's room. That's the only time I was helpful to you, the only time I felt loved by you. Somehow, that became all that I had to offer you. If it wasn't Charlie's room or giving you the money that Charlie gave me, you didn't notice me; I was invisible to you. Your 'babygirl' was nothing but a money-making sex machine to you. Mama, what happened to the good times we would spend watching all of your favorite shows in the trailer park. I mean, we would watch Courage the Cowardly Dog, Ed Ed and Eddy, Charmed, Law & Order, Jaws, and Terminator on weekends when you were home. Why couldn't we build off of that relationship as I continued to get older? Why did you stop caring about having a bond with me?

Life must've surpassed kicking your ass for you to sell your own daughter. You were supposed to protect me, but you put me in the most danger. You were supposed to love me unconditionally, care deeply for me, and you were incapable. Your incapability to provide me with the love I needed introduced me to a life of hell searching for it.

I used to wonder if saying no was an option. If I said no, I didn't know what would happen to me? Then I realized it wouldn't just be what would happen to me, but all of us. I knew we probably wouldn't have a place to stay, ride to school, food, and you would be so hostile if you were unable to fund your addiction.

Once I felt like I had a voice, I escaped you and Charlie's room for a long time. Bouncing around with different relatives seemed better than constantly feeling obligated to have sex with a wrinkled man so you can get high. I wonder if I escaped sooner than 11 years old, I'd be different or better. Maybe I would have had more confidence, or I wouldn't have allowed so many people to mishandle and mistreat me. The responsibility, guilt, and shame were so heavy to carry. At such a young age, I should have never felt so burdened by my own thoughts and questions. The most relevant question was, why me? It was the very question that would haunt me for years to come.

Chapter two
WHAT YOU TAUGHT ME

The mistakes you made while being present in my life were actually a present. Some of your mistakes made me too cautious because I never wanted to be like you. Every day I watched you be a woman that I never wanted to become. Sometimes I wonder what kind of woman I would've become if I had a role model in you or even a friend, someone I could be open to so I don't make the same mistakes.

I remember when you used to take us with you to clean Ned's house. Except, my siblings and I were doing all of the cleaning. You probably didn't know we could hear you upstairs having sex with him. Did you really think we were that stupid?

Ned gave you everything you needed, a ride, drug money, food, everything you asked him for. Was it really worth the trade of your body though? Ned knew you had us, but I wonder if he knew that he was enabling your addiction. Maybe he knew but just didn't care as long as he was getting cheap sex. See Mama, that's not love. He didn't care about you because he was supporting the very thing that was hindering you.

Then there was Timothy; I could not freaking stand Timothy. I can't believe you let him stay with you. I can't believe I had to come back and live with you while he was there. He was a sorry excuse for a man. All he did was get high with you and stress you out. Do you really think you loved him, or he loved you? If he loved you, he would have loved the very things that you created.

Do you remember the day I told you that he put his hands on me? I can't believe I had to defend myself against an entire grown man. Your man. When I told you, you didn't even care. Somehow he was still allowed to stay in the house, which meant I had to go.

Between all of your baby daddies and your failed situationships, you also showed me how I did not want my love life to be. I mean, you would have a boyfriend but still have sex with other men for money. And watching you just give the most precious part of yourself away for a few dollars has made it so hard for me to accept money from men.

Transactional love is what you taught me. For the longest time, my brain was programmed to think that I would only be loved if I had something to give. Do you know how much this has fucked me over? The only time I got love from you was when I had something to give you, so I over gave myself to everyone in return for friendships and relationships. Out here just over giving everything I got because I was so desperate to get the treatment I was giving. On the bright side, you taught me to only aim for marriage and to only have kids with one person.

The first time I saw you burning that glass crack pipe between your lips, I was speechless. I watched your lips move in and out uncontrollably. It silenced you. No one would hear from you for hours.

Whenever I smelled Pine Sol and heard R&B, I knew you were high. The best time to get a yes out of you was when you were high. You would be in a completely different world that you didn't care what we would do. The amount of freedom I had was insane. Luckily I was a smart girl, or I really would have ended up just like you.

Your addiction made me scared to ever be hooked on anything. I've had my moments with marijuana, though. Honestly, I love weed. I would use it to cope with depression, though I was probably making it worse sometimes. That habit was always short-lived. I'd only smoke for a week straight on and off because I was afraid of being codependent. It also caused me to feel more shame. Everyone smoked weed, but oftentimes I hid that I smoked because of my negative connotation with drugs. I thought that people would look at me the way I looked at you, weak. Then I would have to see myself for who I was. Was I a hypocrite? Did I justify my drug use because I would always stop? If we're being completely honest, I would only stop because I would think of you. Thinking of all those times when we lacked financially, still you did anything to get high. Visualizing you at only 30 but missing your teeth was disturbing. Watching you be so naive and easily manipulated by men just to get the Heroine was disappointing. I knew that wasn't how I wanted to show up in this world. So, as a matter of fact, you saved me from addiction.

Everything that you taught me wasn't all bad either. Yes, I learned a lot about who I absolutely did not want to be, but you are more than your flaws. You chased the wrong things in life but your determination to get it was commendable. Mama, girl, if it meant you had to walk from the trailer park in Chester all the way to Richmond, you were going to get what you needed. Chester to Richmond was about a thirty-minute drive. My favorite part was when you would let me walk with you, and we'd stop at the store for a Take 5 candy bar. We used to love those things. You're a by any means necessary type of woman. I love that about you.

Another thing you passed to me is the value of always having a spotless house. I'm exactly like you because I don't play about my house being dirty. I light candles, play some good ole Mary J. Blidge, and get lost in the aroma of cleaning supplies. Cleaning has been by far the best coping mechanism for me, before I found fitness. Now listen, you cannot cook. You're good with the hamburger helper, which was my absolute favorite, but you can only be trusted with the easy stuff. Do you remember teaching me how to peel and cut potatoes? Being your helper was my favorite part about you cooking. It was one of my favorite times being around you. The one moment where I felt like I was learning something good from you.

Mama, I wanted to look up to you so bad. I craved having that loving mother-daughter relationship with you. The few years that I had to live with you caused me so much pain that I never wanted to experience it again. Because I never wanted to be associated with your image, I lived my life fixated on creating a life opposite of yours. My goals were to never be addicted to anything, have only one baby daddy who would also be my loving husband, and never be codependent. Having you as an example was both favorable and detrimental to my growth. Favorable because I knew not to follow in your footsteps, yet detrimental because I could never be myself trying not to be you. Your absence blessed me more than you know, but it also hindered me. Little did I know, no matter how hard I tried not to be like you, I would fall into the exact things I hated most about you.

Chapter three
GROWING UP WITHOUT YOU

A lot of events transpired over the years that you have no clue about. I mean, the last time I lived with you was for a few weeks in Mosby Court projects. The roaches were outrageous, so I had to go. Then I lived with Ma in her hotel room for a few weeks. I'm not even sure if you knew where I was.

Bouncing around a lot was hard because I could never find myself, especially after having to leave Emporia with Aunt Joyce in the middle of 7th grade. I had a best friend and even had made the cheerleading squad. After all the craziness that I'd been through, I thought I could finally be normal like everyone else. Then Aunt Joyce thought I was having sex and got rid of me. Well, at least that's what I think is why I truly don't know. Might've been influenced by the wrong people, but I wasn't having sex.

I begged our cousin Lena to take me in. Only because I thought she had a normal family, and that's what I craved. For once, I wanted to be in a household with two financially stable parents. Parents that cared about my future and pushed me to do more. I wanted to show up at school looking like someone cared about me. I needed to get home from school and have someone care about how school went. Lena provided clean clothes, family dinners, and a better environment than what I was used to. But child, little did I know, she would be the cousin from hell.

Lena was crazy. One time she had bought me a two-piece bathing suit, and when I wore it, she made me throw it away. I could only wear tankinis. This was so embarrassing because even my little cousins wore two-piece bathing suits. This actually made me so self-conscious. Due to everything I've already experienced sexually, I already didn't fit in. When she singled me out, it made me feel like everyone else knew about those encounters with Charlie.

Lena had 4 sons, and one was a newborn. Most nights, he would be with me unless I was on punishment. He was really fussy from colic, but he did well with me for some reason. A baby's love is unconditional, so I didn't mind taking care of him. I would wake up to change him, make his bottle, and put him back to sleep. I loved him so much. Every time he would smile or stop crying when I held him, I felt loved back.

Every day after I got out of school, I would have to hurry home to make lunch for the other boys and clean the entire apartment. I had a little more than an hour to clean the bathrooms, kitchen, everyone's bedroom, sweep, vacuum, and cook. After I was done with everything, I had to go get them from the bus stop, feed them and help them do their homework before she got home from work. Basically, I needed to take care of all of her responsibilities so that she could do nothing when she was done driving buses.

I respected her boyfriend Mike, though. He worked as a chef. When he got home from work, he would hang out with his sons and cook us dinner. It was hard being super comfortable around Mike because of my experiences with Charlie but also because I didn't have a relationship with my dad. No matter how much Mike tried to interact with me, I just didn't know how to accept him. I appreciated him, though, a lot. It was never his intention to make me feel uncomfortable. He wanted me to feel like his daughter; he treated me like his daughter. Lena used to say that I was the daughter she never had, but the longer I stayed, the more I realized that she didn't have my best interest at heart.

Lena used to do things that were so humiliating, harsh even. Whenever she would punish me, she would take away my flat iron, makeup kit, earrings, and all of my newer clothes and shoes just so I could go to school looking raggedy. She would even unplug the cable box in my room. I never cared when she said I couldn't go outside because I could almost never go outside anyway.

I remember trying out for the cheerleading team at Lucille Brown Middle School, and not only did I make the team, but I also made captain. Do you know why this woman didn't let me cheer? She thought the uniform was inappropriate. I was 12; the uniform was just fine. Cheerleading was probably the only thing that made me feel normal. It gave me a sense of belonging. How else was I going to make friends? How else would I fit in? No matter how hard I would try to fit in, I was still the girl whose mom sold her for drugs. The girl whose parents didn't love her. The girl who was only 12 but had already had her first sexual encounter.

Living with Lena made things a lot worse for me. I felt like Cinderella there; I guess that's why I ran away. Never had a real sense of belonging. I was an outcast at school and at home. All I wanted was to be loved, but I experienced transactional love once again. If I wasn't of any benefit to her, she did not love me. Before I knew that the only reason she took me in was to collect child support from my dad and increase her food stamps, I actually thought she might care. I thought she would be the woman who wanted better for me. I thought that she would be a better role model for me. Instead, I found myself in the household of another broken woman.

I didn't see her then, but I see who she is now. A woman who has been broken. A woman who lost herself. I know how insecure she was because of the way she used to talk about other women. Projection is something else.

After Lena, I ended up right back with you for the first time in so many years. I was fourteen and a freshman in high school. Back with you meant back to Charlie's house. This time was different, though. You never asked me to go into Charlie's room, and neither did he. While you would think this was a blessing for me, it wasn't. Believe me when I say I never wanted those things to happen to me. Of course, I didn't want to do it, but something about him not wanting me made me feel even lower. It made me wonder if something was wrong with me.

A couple of weeks into staying with you and Charlie, my dad was on the doorstep to pick me up. Now, this came as a total shock to me. I mean, I barely knew the man. I could count on my hands how many times I have seen him my whole life. Why would you do that to me? Why didn't you ask me if I wanted to go stay with him? Why didn't you want me there with you? Or was it Charlie who didn't want me there? The most hurtful part was you switching my school behind my back. This meant I had to deal with the anxiety of being the new girl all over again.

I went from Huguenot high school to George Wythe high school at the end of my freshman year. This school transition was the hardest of them all. Kids were way crueler in high school. Everyone always knew when there was a new girl, and I didn't want anyone to know me. I used to wish I could just hide. Maybe that's why I didn't talk to anyone, and I sped walked from one class to the next. That made things worse because, to the girls, I was stuck up.

So, here I am, once again, the outcast. I figured I should just do what I've always done and join different organizations. This would earn me a few acquaintances and also keep me out of the home you forced me into. Before I knew it, I was a part of the soccer team, track & field, cheerleading, FCCLA (Family Career & Community Leaders of America, NHS (National Honors Society), Ladylike, and so many others that I know I'm missing a few. As if that wasn't enough, I also had got a job at Krogers and braided hair on the weekends. Anything to stay away from the awkwardness of being around my dad.

It was bad enough that I never had your support in anything, but not having his presence or attention was probably worse. I mean, we lived right behind the school. Our games were visible from the backyard, and he came to one game, and only stayed for twenty minutes. All of the award ceremonies, games, meets, and he wouldn't even ask about it. This was when I really learned that I would probably never get the stable household full of love and support that I truly desired.

On March 4, 2014, I thought I was going to have a great day of rest. School had been closed due to the snow. If I had been home alone, it would have been even better, but I was snowed in with his wife's daughter. Now, I didn't have a relationship with her like I did with her mother. I kind of envied her in a sense. She was a spoiled brat. Her mom bought her whatever she wanted, she lived in a two-parent household, visited her dad on the weekends, and her mom was at all of her events. All her mom used to ask her to do was clean her room, and she couldn't even do that. The little girl was so disrespectful. It reminded me of the time when I was around her age, maybe 8, and we were on the way to Emporia. I was distraught in the backseat, full of tears because I had left my library book at home. You must have been having a really bad day because you pulled your heel off and smacked fire from me. I never expected that from you. But to think that I was a straight-A student, respectful, and responsible never got me the attention I sought was mind-boggling to me. I thought, damn, what do I have to do? Should I have been disrespectful like her? When will someone notice all of my achievements? When will someone notice how much I'm hurting? Will anyone ever notice that I need unconditional love? Maybe not, but soon everyone would know exactly what happened to me.

This snow day that I thought would be so relaxing, locked in my room alone, I woke up to his wife's daughter telling me that she smelled smoke. I was going to ignore her because I did not like her, but something told me not to. I realized if she was talking to me, she must've been serious.

I rolled out of bed to check it out, and lo and behold, the master bedroom was full of dark smoke. Now, I have never in my life seen this before. I'm still not quite sure why I would keep walking in there to figure out what was causing it, but all I could do was choke. Shout out to my instincts again because my next reaction was to get her and the dog and get the hell out of there. We went next door to the neighbor's house to wait while she called my dad and his wife.

After a few seconds of standing in the neighbor's doorway, we watch the roof burst into flames. Once the firefighters were done, we had lost everything. From there, we lived in a hotel for a few weeks until we were placed in an apartment. Would you believe that I was in school the next day like nothing ever happened? I had got picked on for having new clothes. They used to say, "She wouldn't even have that if her house didn't burn down."

After the house burned down, I really wished I was invisible. Stability was non-existent, living out of trash bags and not having home-cooked meals. The agonizing stares and whispers at school were so damn annoying. It seemed like I was damned if I do and damned if I don't.

They talked about me for not having the best clothes and talked about me when I had newer clothes. I mean, so many people donated, I didn't have to really repeat clothes much anymore. How was that my fault?

With all of the stress at home and school, my mental health started declining. A few days after the fire, I broke down crying in the hallway. My principal found me and made me speak to one of the counselors at the school. Talking to her might have been one of the biggest turning points in my life.

Discussing the molestation, your addiction, and circumstances growing up was always a fear of mine. Not to protect you, but my younger sisters. While I didn't want those things happening to them, I didn't want them to be in the system either. I figured it would always be best if I just kept trying to act like nothing ever happened.

It was too big of a secret for me; I guess that's why I finally spit it out. While tears were profusely running down my face, and I could barely speak over all of the gasping, I told her everything. Well, almost everything; I never went into the details about the sexual abuse. I didn't know how to say my mom sold me, so I just said I was raped.

Gosh, I felt so alleviated. Speaking out took so much burden off of my back. I would be able to walk around about fifty pounds lighter. That was until after I was done crying. I could not believe I told her everything because she had to report it by law. So much anxiety came over me when I realized you might find out what I had done. Thoughts bolted through my mind for days about how much you would hate me. I was afraid Child Protective Services would come to get my sisters. I didn't even think about the conversation that I may have to have with my dad. As I write this, I wonder if you'll hate me for it. If so, I truly apologize; what is inside of me must come out.

My dad seemed like he cared when the counselor initially told him what I had confessed. He seemed like he felt bad because he wasn't there. For a couple of weeks, I had finally got the compassion that I wanted and needed.

The counselor had recommended therapy, so I had started going to a place called Child Savers. My therapist was a middle-aged white man. I didn't know how therapy with him would help me because my abuser was an older white man.

Normally, I didn't always speak up for myself, so I never said that I didn't feel comfortable talking to him. Besides, most of the things he would ask were pretty surface level. We only had two sessions alone before having a session with my dad present. I remember the therapist asked a question about my childhood, and I mentioned step-daddy, Aaliyah's dad, and therapy was over in a blink of an eye. My dad was so enraged about that because I never called him dad or daddy. Typically, I would just start talking, so I didn't call him anything. I really wasn't sure what I did wrong. How was it my fault that step-daddy was there when I was a child, and he wasn't? Step-daddy was also there before I was consistently being molested and raped. Therefore, I was more comfortable with him.

The reality of the situation was that I didn't really know my dad. That's why I am not sure why you forced me to go live with him. Since everything happened, I have never been comfortable around older men. I view them all the same, whether they are related to me or not, especially if I don't know them well. I used to imagine how different my life would be if I had a better relationship with my dad. Maybe I would have never been sexually abused. I would imagine that he would have been able to protect me and provide for me. If he was providing, then I wouldn't have felt like I had no choice but to provide for you. Maybe I wouldn't have such low self-esteem or lust after validation from the opposite sex.

By the time my dad tried to play a father role in my life, which he had sucked at, I no longer needed him. It was like he missed the mark. I had already lost my virginity at 14. Well, not virginity, but I had consensual sex. He never really talked to me about anything important in life or asked about mine. I still had to fend for myself. I knew he didn't care about all the past trauma I told him about because he pulled me out of therapy. Just wasn't really sure why he wanted to be in my life when he wasn't doing anything for me. Family members said he attained custody of me so that he wouldn't have to pay child support any longer. Not sure if it's true, but I wouldn't be surprised. Just more transactional love.

We already didn't have a relationship, but things went downhill even more after the therapy session. I think I was so frustrated that yet another person who said they loved me didn't show it. At some point, I had lost all respect for him. I remember that he took the door off of the hinges to my room because he didn't like that I would stay in my room with the door shut. I hated living with him so much. He tried so hard to control me. He didn't realize that at fifteen years old, I no longer needed a parent; I only needed guidance. I had already been doing everything on my own, so I didn't need anyone to tell me what to do. In his mind, I guess I was going down the wrong path, but I was certain about my future. I always have been. With all of the things that I had going for myself, I'm not even sure why he thought that. Maybe he saw you in me. Everyone says you used to be a smart, pretty girl. You think he was scared I would be just like you?

At some point, he ended up admitting me to the crisis stabilization unit at St. Joseph's Villa. There was absolutely no need for me to go there.

He probably thought it was punishment, but I honestly enjoyed my two-week stay. The counselors were super nice. We played all kinds of games and did some fun activities. This is where I drew my rose tattoo. One flower was black, which represented my past, and one that was colored to represent my flourishing future.

Although I couldn't communicate with anyone or see anyone, I was fine with that. This was the first time I was diagnosed with depression. My dad's wife refused the medication that they wanted to put me on. I was upset because they claimed they sent me there for help but then refused the help. The truth is, they just wanted me out of the house. Which I knew was true because a couple of weeks after finally being released from the crisis unit, I was right back with you. And when all of this happened, I knew to never speak on anything ever again. You had told me that he said I was not welcome in his new house. I felt like I was being punished for finally telling the truth about everything.

Living with you was not what was best for me. You were 30 minutes away from my school, and there was no way I was going to switch schools again. Thankfully, I was close enough with my dad's next-door neighbor Mani who let me stay with her. Staying there wasn't perfect. I slept on the couch, so still no real stability. Her mother and 3 sons also lived in the small 3 bedroom.

On the bright side, though, I finally was getting the attention I needed. She treated me like the daughter she never had. However, she was barely thirty, so I looked at her more like a sister.

Things were great until they weren't anymore. I don't remember much of what happened, but I know I was in yet another broken home. No real guidance, stability, love, or structure.

My only option at this point was my best friend's house. I met her at Huguenot in ninth grade and we kind of kept in touch. I would stay with her, and my friend Quannie would give me a ride to school in the morning. I'd catch the bus from school to work and figure it out from there. While I had a plan, I really was uncertain how it was going to work out. I loved my best friend, but she was crazy. Her whole family was crazy. She lived with her mom, aunt, and younger brother. Sometimes we would come home from school, and her mom would yell at us about buying toilet paper. She would find stuff to yell about. My best friend would sometimes go off on her mom, and I would be so scared. I was scared for my best friend but scared that we would both get kicked out because I was on my last option.

Then one day, my best friend and I got into a fight. She had pulled a knife out on me and probably would've really stabbed me if her brother didn't get there in time. We had made up, but shortly after, her mom did the same thing you did. My dad was at the door one day telling me to get my stuff.

Staying with my dad again did not last long. Everything was still the same. I hated him for who I knew him to be, which was a liar and someone who wasn't there for me. You and my grandma told me that he introduced you to drugs. When I asked him about it after therapy, he denied all of it. However, I knew who he was already. I saw it with my own eyes. I'm not sure if he was the real reason, but I knew he wasn't as innocent as he tried to make himself seem.

Although I wasn't eighteen, I was very much an adult. I had been on my own. So I hated that he treated me like a child, trying to shelter me from the truth. I'm sure hiding the truth was for his reputation and not my protection. Question, if you knew he was just as much of an addict as you, why would you send me with him?

One night I was lying down listening to music in my room. My door was open because he wouldn't let me shut it. My dad came to the doorway and asked me to turn my music off because his stepdaughter needed to go to sleep. I told him to just shut my door. Now, I know I probably shouldn't have said that but what is the harm in shutting my door? What could I possibly be doing in that tiny house with my door shut? Solitude brought me peace. Sometimes I needed to just be alone and think. Maybe if he took the time to talk to me about my life, then he would have understood that.

He came into my room and tried to snatch my phone out of my hand. That led to a physical altercation because I was not about to let him take something that I purchased and paid for with the job he wouldn't even give me a ride to. He was shoving me, pushing me; I couldn't believe it, honestly. When I broke loose, I called the police. Next thing you know, his sister was there yelling in my face calling me a bitch. They both made me pack my stuff and dropped me off in Petersburg at your house. I didn't even get a chance to shut the door all the way before he sped off.

Chapter four
NOT WITH YOU AGAIN

I wasn't mad about having to leave his house; I was mad about having to come to your house. I was worried about how I would get to school every day. I was in the middle of my senior year and was not about to ruin my GPA. Luckily for me, the mother figure I had been wishing for in you, I had found in my teachers at school. I had one teacher, Ms. Artis, who lived near you and would let me ride with her in the mornings. My assistant cheerleading coach, Ms. Gardner, would also help out as much as she could. But there were so many other reasons I couldn't live with you. I didn't know how to keep pretending like nothing ever happened. We also just didn't have the relationship we needed to have. Another thing, that house was not up to par. Why did you think you could hide that you had bed bugs? I couldn't sleep on that small couch and keep getting bitten up like that every night. It was so bad that I found myself sleeping on top of my container that had my clothes in it some nights. One day at school, I noticed a bed bug crawling out of my book bag. Now imagine how much worse I would have been talked about. I was already different enough.

Ms. Gardner ended up being my rock and still is. She let me stay with her, so I didn't have to stay with you. That's how I knew she really cared for me because, at the time, she was staying with her dad. Even still, she opened up her space to me. She was a mother, sister, and best friend all in one. There was nothing I couldn't talk to her about. We never talked about all of the sexual abuse and whatnot, but I knew I could if I needed to.

You don't know this, but there was one night that you let me leave, and I stayed at a guy's house. Since I was a freshman, I'd known him, but this was the first time I had sex with him. It was also the first time I got pregnant. I never told you because I knew you were going to make me keep it. We had just had a conversation a few days before where I asked you what you would have done if I had gotten pregnant. With everything I had going for myself, the type of guy he was, and the fact that I really loved someone else, I knew I couldn't have a baby. Where would we even live? Ms. Gardner told me we would figure it out together whatever my decision was, and I believed her. She was trustworthy. She kept my secret from all of the other cheerleaders, teachers, and even you.

Being that I was under 18, I had to go see a judge to get permission to get an abortion. The process of everything took so long I was almost 14 weeks pregnant by the time I could have the procedure.

I was given nausea medication and medication for my Rh-negative blood type at the start of my appointment. A few other ladies were in the waiting area with me. They all looked much older, though. There was one younger black girl who looked around my age. When I saw her, I thought, at least, I'm not alone. Until I saw her mother come sit next to her and hold her hand. In reality, I was alone. Yeah, Ms. Gardner was there with me, but it just wasn't the same. Having to keep another secret and going through another traumatic event so young was a lot.

The medication they gave me started to make me feel ill. The next thing I knew, I was vomiting in front of everyone. Once I started crying, I knew it couldn't get any worse. I couldn't figure out why I was crying. What made me so emotional? Was it that I felt guilty for what I was doing? Or maybe I felt so much shame and embarrassment since I was only 17. Because there was no way I actually grew an attachment for a baby I didn't want, right? If only you were capable of supporting me that day. You could have told me how to handle it since you have been down that road before. I wish I could have trusted you to be there for me, but I'm so grateful that I had someone who was. You should be too.

Sometimes, I wonder why didn't you abort me. Ma said you were so strung out on drugs that everyone thought I would be born with defects. You and my dad weren't together, and he even made you get a paternity test. You were nineteen years old with a three and four-year-old. You had already been married, still were. So what was your thought processing on having yet another kid that you were unsuited to care for?

Lying on that cold table with my feet propped up, uncontrollably sobbing, was one of the most humiliating feelings. I felt like a statistic. The doctors had to have thought I was just another black girl going down the wrong path. They probably thought I was so foolish. I was proving everyone right about me, that I would be just like you. There was no amount of medicine that could have fixed the amount of pain that I was in both emotionally and physically. To think that this would be my first of many abortions.

Your hurtfulness came in doses over the years. Each dose showed me over and over who you were. It wasn't unlike you to run after half-ass men; I knew this about you. I've watched you settle for so many things. I'm sure it is because you never thought that you could have more. I'm sure no one ever told you that you deserve more, besides maybe Sleepy. Sometimes I imagine how your life would be different if he was still alive.

At some point, you were at least halfway trying to get clean. When I was maybe eight years old, I remember you would go to the methadone clinic most mornings. I wasn't sure if it would ever work since you would still do drugs. What I did know was that you were trying. In order to try, you have to have some kind of want or hope for change. You must've envisioned something better for yourself. What were your dreams, Mama? Why did you keep losing hope? Was it hard for you to watch me go after mine because you didn't go after yours?

Packing up your life to follow behind your unworthy boyfriend a day before my graduation had to have been one of your highest doses of hurt. Even if you did make a move, was it too much to ask you to drive four hours to come see me walk across the stage? Graduation is one of the biggest milestones in your child's life. Besides, do you know how hard it was to make it through high school? I was a loner most of the time because I never knew how to fit in, which I didn't realize until later was a gift. My only friends were a few of the basketball players because my cheating boyfriend was on the team. I was a part of teams and organizations but didn't know how to build friendships, so I would still find myself alone. Everyone else in the school bullied me for being 'stuck up,' not knowing that I really wasn't. On top of all that, I suffered severe anxiety and depression. Walking across that stage with all of my awards and recognitions gave me confidence. It made me proud. I knew that if I could get through those challenging years, I could get through anything that was to come.

I thought I would at least make you proud. Maybe I could have given you a sense of relief, knowing that good things can come from you. When you left, I never heard from you again. The least you could have done was called to say congratulations. You could have shown me that you cared a little bit. When you missed graduation, and I didn't hear from you, that was my excuse to never speak to you again.

Luckily, I was surrounded by a few people who did care about my accomplishment. Mainly Ms. Gardner. Since I had met her, she has been there every step of the way. She was there when I walked across the stage, went off to college, walked down the aisle, dropped out of college, and even when I moved to New Mexico. All of the things you missed, she was there for.

Chapter five

NAVIGATING TOXIC RELATIONSHIPS

My love life has been the biggest threat to my overall health, especially as an adult. There were so many abusive situations. My marriage crumbling was the rippling effect to all of my future situationships.

Since transactional love had been all I knew, I was easy to take advantage of. This led me to a life of settling for breadcrumbs, thinking that I didn't deserve better. Thinking that I couldn't have better and that I should be satisfied with the fact that someone wanted me. Instead, I should have loved myself so much that I knew my worth so that I could attract what I deserve and repel what was not for me.

Whenever someone finds out I got married at 18, the first question is 'why?' I never know how to answer this question. The second question is, 'were we in the military? The answer to that is an easy no. I just say because we were in love. Never have I ever been sure about this answer. Yes, my ex-husband was my best friend, but the lying and cheating started way before we got married. It started all the way in high school. So if we're being completely honest, I don't know why I got married.

I mean, throughout high school, he felt like the only person I had, even if he was deceiving. He used to hurt me so badly; it was so humiliating. Girls would message me all kinds of proof of his cheating, including actual pictures. I can't believe I stuck around for this type of behavior. It wasn't like I didn't have options; I was just stuck on him, more like stuck on stupid.

He knew a lot about me, but I had never gone into details about most things, especially not the rape. He knew more about the relationship with my dad than you because that's where I was living. I even lived with him a lot in high school. His parents had a tiny two-bedroom low-income apartment where almost the whole family stayed. Sometimes we would sleep on a mattress in the living because the couches and bedrooms were already taken.

Living with him was not the most ideal situation, but his home was full of love. He had a two-parent household and even had relationships with his siblings. Did you ever think about how important it was for my siblings and me to have relationships? We have been split up for so long it seems weird to rekindle anything. We don't really know each other. My oldest siblings have different mindsets than I do. Sometimes, I just don't understand why they don't want more for themselves. We grew up in the same environments, yet they are comfortable. I've always been uncomfortable with my youngest siblings being with you, but I know that is out of my control. I wish you had taken more control over trying to keep us together so that we at least had each other.

The worst part about it, though, is that I am the one that is isolated. My oldest sister and brother live together now and have always had a relationship, maybe because they have the same dad. Of course, the younger two are with you. Then there is me, always alone.

Since you lost one brother to a car accident, one to the system, and a sister to domestic violence, you know how it feels to be apart. Was it hard losing your siblings? Was it a fear of yours that we would all lose each other? Did you ever care about us having each other's back?

Anyway, it was nice becoming a part of his family. Ironically, I was never uncomfortable around his dad. He was so genuine to me; his brothers were too. My ex-husband had a sister who didn't like me, but I tried to tune it out.

It's like he showed up for me as if he really cared about my well-being in front of my face but disowned me behind my back. I wish I had you to talk to about everything before I got married.

Remember how I said I strived so hard not to be like you. The truth is that I had such low self-esteem, I probably would've married just about any man that wanted to marry me just to feel better about myself. Having a husband meant someone saw some value in me at the time. It meant that I would have someone to protect and not abandon me.

Marriage was a big accomplishment for me. Whenever I would accomplish these unrealistic life expectations I placed over myself to not be like you, I felt comfort. The downside was when I failed at this because I would lose hope. I would lose hope that I could have a better life than you did.

Everyone around us supported this marriage. I'm not sure if it was genuine or because no one wanted to speak up. His parents had been married for a long time. It was surprising they didn't tell us to wait. Why didn't anyone say how hard it would be? How come no one thought it was a good idea to speak up? Where were you?

After I dropped out of Old Dominion University freshman year, we got married that summer. Most of our marriage was spent in New Mexico. He was going there for a spot on the basketball team at school. We had been long-distance for so long it wasn't working anymore.

After six months at my job, I was allowed to work remotely. As soon as I received my equipment, I packed my entire car up and drove twenty-six hours to New Mexico alone. The drive started roughly; I had a panic attack driving at 4 am in the rain. It was pitch black outside, there were no other cars on the road, and all I could see were shadows and trees. I was being attacked by all of the negative thoughts ramming in my head. What if I crash? What if this is a bad idea? What if I get lost? I was blowing up my husband's phone because I just needed someone to tell me that everything would be okay. I didn't know what was to come from this decision, and that scared the shit out of me. The only thing that kept me going was the fact that I had faith in the person I was going to be with. I had faith in my happily ever after. I'd go through anything to get it, even if that meant navigating through states alone for the first time.

I remember all of the times that I needed you to tell me that everything was going to be okay. Like when I had my first period at school in 7th grade or when I was away at college losing my mind. Those times in New Mexico were when I needed you the most.

We would argue so much until he would just walk out on me. I never understood why he would be so angry at me as if I was the one who cheated. Then as if cheating was enough for my self-esteem, he would place my abandonment issues on display by walking out while I was trying to be heard. All I wanted was to be heard and seen. Everything was about him. I worked over 100 hours, drove hours to make all of his games and lost myself in it. I didn't know who I was anymore. My whole life revolved around being a good wife and supporting my husband. It didn't help that I no longer noticed myself physically either. I had gained seventy pounds. Two hundred pounds was the heaviest I had ever been in my life. Maybe that's why he cheated this time? But why did he cheat all the other times? Why would I marry someone who was always a liar and cheater?

I loved that man so much. I lost myself in him. Ever since we met in high school, he has been my best friend. He was my rainbow in the storm. He waited to have sex with me and even opened his home to me. I thought he had my best interest at heart.

Over the years, I never felt appreciated by him. How could you cheat on the person who drove twenty-six hours across the country to be with you? How could you lie to the person who always told you everything? How could you disrespect the person that bought you whatever you wanted?

Those times where I would get in my own head trying to answer unanswered questions were when I needed you to be there. The first time I couldn't stop hearing that no one loved me. I couldn't shake the feeling of alienation and feeling like no one cared. I needed you to tell me it was all going to be okay. I needed you to talk me out of that closet. I needed you to grab the bottle of pills out of my hand. I needed you to wipe my tears, hug me, and teach me how to leave a situation that was no longer serving me.

When I called you, the first thing you said was, 'what are you crying for?' It was more so how you said it that pushed me closer to the edge. You said it like I shouldn't be crying. You said it as if I was bothering you. Truth be told, I don't know why I called you. Our relationship was over at this point because I got tired of you asking for money without even asking how I was doing. Could you really not tell that I was going through it when I called you? You made me feel so stupid for calling, so I just hung up. You were the last person I called that day. When you didn't call back, I took the whole bottle of pain medication.

It was twenty-eight pills, to be exact. They were supposed to stop the thoughts and make the anxiety go away. Instead, I was completely still in the closet, wondering if it was going to work. I was trying to convince myself that even after finally being calm, I still wanted to die so that I won't regret what I had done. Since you never called back and my husband never answered after I told him what I was going to do, it still seemed like the right decision to make.

Today I'm thankful that I'm still here, but then I was so mad nothing happened. So mad that I would attempt suicide again. It started the same way; he walked out during the fight. This time was different, though. Even though I was cutting up my wrist, he still walked out. There was no way he loved me. Why didn't he stop me instead? Was it just too much for him to deal with? The truth is, before he left, I didn't want to die; I wanted him to care so much that he stopped me. After he left, I wish I had a better way to get it over with.

No matter how dark my world would get, I still had access to the voice that told me to keep going. There was a quieter voice that reminded me to look at my accomplishments. It would tell me that if I got this far, I could keep going. That whisper has been the only thing that saved me at my lowest points. I just needed to learn how to make this voice drown out the one telling me to give up. Do you have a voice in your head that tells you to do better? Do you have a voice that tells you to be better?

Eventually, I got myself together. I started to focus more on what I wanted out of life. So I re-enrolled into college, stopped working so much, and took control of my health. Before you know it, I was back down to one hundred-forty pounds and couldn't wait to leave his ass in New Mexico.

The divorce ruined my fairytale. It stole my hope that I could be better than you. I carried so much shame because I knew marrying him was a bad idea deep down. When I got out of the marriage, I was so unfamiliar with myself. Pretending was a natural thing for me. Everyone around me probably thought I was just fine. In reality, I came back from New Mexico, ten times more hurt than when I went.

I'm certain he didn't realize that not seeing me for so long was pushing me away. He probably thought I was leaving him for the cheating, which was valid. I used to think that it was okay to get cheated on. Everyone says 'every man cheats,' and that's one of the reasons I would always stay. That, and the fact that I was so desperate for love. While I was starved of honesty, loyalty, respect, and unconditional love, I kept waiting for it to be returned.

After I left New Mexico, I did go back for his graduation. I felt like I had to show up for him because that's what I would always do. Besides, I still hoped that he would get it together one day.

When he came back to Virginia, he lived with his parents, and I had an apartment close by. I helped him get a job and everything. We called ourselves trying again, so I even let the man move in with me. That was very brief because I went through his social accounts and saw he was flirting with at least fifty girls. Even girls that he knew didn't like me. What makes it worse is that he had just been served with child support papers. How in the world was I married to someone who possibly had a five-year-old that no one knew about? I even went with him to take the DNA test, just riding and dying. Until this day, I still don't know what happened with that situation. He says that it was dropped.

So many crazy things transpired between us. Like the time he called the police on me to take my car, or the time he crawled up onto my balcony after I had kicked him out. So much crazy stuff that I was exhausted. I just couldn't take it anymore.

We got divorced in December 2020. I was married for two years to the person I thought I'd spend forever with. Honestly, it wasn't what I wanted to do, but it felt like I needed to. I needed to give up hope that he would get himself together. The story between us is never ending though because up until today, he picks up whenever I call.

I had never taken the time to heal from the marriage. So not only was I looking to fill the void of not having you or my dad, now I was seeking validation from losing my husband. Marriage validated me. If someone wanted to marry me, I was something, right?

41

It took so many more failed relationships for me to understand that I actually didn't have to give anything to be loved. It took the man with who I wasn't in a relationship with to get me pregnant.

After that first abortion, I promised God and myself that I would never do it again. My mind was so made up, which meant the guy hated me. He told me I would be just like you, that my child would grow up just like me, and that every nigga hurt me because my dad wasn't there. He asked me, 'what kind of mother do you think you are going to be?' He shot at my ego with that one. I didn't know myself enough to know what kind of mother I would be. All I ever thought about was what kind of wife I would be. Did you ever picture yourself as a mom? What did that look like for you? What was the reason you wanted to be a mom? The only positive thing I could find about becoming a mom was providing for it. Like every other girl my age that just wanted to go buy cute baby clothes. I knew I would teach my baby, but I never thought about the lessons disguised as a calamity that would help her. I never thought about teaching her what love is, who God is, and who she is. I never thought about it because I didn't know for myself yet.

Is it true that maybe you never knew what love was, who God is, and who you are? Have you ever wanted to find out? I would see your Godly post on Facebook, but have you ever wanted to dive deeper than that?

Lord knows I did. Depression had its arms hugging me so tightly. I couldn't shake it; It was so heavy. I felt so alone. I felt like everyone could see how much weight I was carrying around that they would distance themselves from me. Even my clientele would slow up in business.

When isolation became the only option, I found someone who loved all parts of me. Even the really jacked-up parts that I was too ashamed to talk about.

I knew that depression couldn't stay clung to me if I could get hugged by God. My faith in knowing that would be tested while I was still trying to meet God where he was. On the way to meeting him, there was no peace. There were unsupportive friends, disrespectful men, a sense of abandonment, loneliness, and my own destructive thoughts.

When I reached a place of stillness, I started questioning myself. I asked, what if you aren't ready for a child? I would just stand in the mirror and think that if I am too depressed to take care of myself, how would I be able to take care of someone else. I would think about how my mood swings, financial irresponsibility, lack of structure, poor time management, and lack of self-love could affect a child, which was also all evidence that I was just like you. Replaying all of those thoughts every day is what led me to the clinic at 14 weeks pregnant.

The third abortion was a no-brainer. I got pregnant by a monster. Looking back at the situation with this man was so pathetic. I had to have been super low on myself to ignore all the red flags that were revealed to me. Like I should have known he was abusive by the way he beat his dog. Every time he smacked or kicked her, my heart would decline to my stomach. The poor dog would be limping the next morning. That was when I first started to be afraid of who he really was. He also didn't respect his mother, but that wasn't a big enough flag for me to leave either. Nor was the first time he had tortured me like he did his dog enough to leave.

The first time he put his hands on me, I was in total disbelief. He was yelling all kinds of derogative insulting slurs at me. He dragged me through every inch of his tiny apartment until the police came. When he did it again, I wish I had told the police everything and pressed charges. The second time he really messed me up, I still have a bad knee. Even though I had to walk with crutches for a few days, I still lied to protect him at the hospital.

I went back after the first time because he convinced me that it was my fault. He convinced me that If I didn't hit him first, he would have never treated me like that. The chokehold he had me in was so secure I believed whatever he would say to me. I started to believe him when he would tell me I was the only one. I believed him until I had no other choice not to. The ex he had cheated with decided to message me that I could have him back. Talking about embarrassment, I was humiliated. This lady was thirty-four, and I'm only twenty-two. She had three kids, and they all lived with her mom. She sounded a lot like you, actually. Man, I didn't know what I had got myself into. It took him to cheat with someone I felt was less than for me to start realizing my worth. I had to remind myself that I was the catch. I wasn't like most women, especially not the ones my age. I always knew I had a bright luxury filled future ahead of me. His cheating switched my perspective from wanting someone to choose me to get selective about who I allow in my life.

Dealing with him is what revealed to me my daddy issues. Ironically, I fell in love with him because of the way he used to treat me.

He came into my life when I was vulnerable. I met him when I was pregnant for the second time. Anything that would make me smile, he did it. He opened doors, cooked for me, bought me flowers, communicated with me, and gave me a sense of protection. He used to always say, 'I know exactly what I'm doing to you; you always gonna love me.' I had no idea what he was talking about until we were over. He was so manipulative. It was like a game for him. He was empowered whenever I was hurt and powerless when he could no longer get to me the same.

What's crazy is I would still check on him after all of that. Not because I wanted to experience a relationship with him again, but because I knew he wasn't okay. I've always had a gift to see people for who they are, whether I accepted it initially or not. I could see right through him. Maybe that's why I dated him anyway; I always think I can fix somebody. Honestly, he needed an exorcism; I had never met someone so dark.

The next guy wasn't a bad person at all, mainly because I started being more selective. I got tired of the fixer-uppers. Things were normal; there was mutual respect, communication, and softness. Through his actions, I could tell that he really cared for me. Our issue was my issue at first. I would romanticize every relationship. I knew I wanted marriage and kids but expressing that made me seem a little crazy. He made it seem like I shouldn't want those things at my age or as if I was doing too much, wanting to plan for my future. I was delusional for wanting to know where the relationship was going next.

Even when I got pregnant by him, I romanticized that too. I thought about the couple we could be, how chocolatey delicious our baby would look, and what kind of life we could build together. Now I know there's nothing wrong with that as long as the other person is on the same page. I wasn't crazy for investing so much of myself and wanting to feel secure. I started to realize he was the crazy one for not seeing what God had put right in front of him.

Things got even worse when he had so many people in his ear telling him what to do. He was not ready for someone like me. I could tell he started to lose himself because he would drink so much. When we met, he said he didn't drink alcohol. We worked because he was just as healthy as me. It wasn't like he was an alcoholic; I could just tell he was in the middle of a battle I knew nothing about. There were parts inside of him that needed healing. At this point in my life, I was no longer interested in healing men while being taken advantage of in the process. I realized that if he wanted to be with me, he would do what he needed to do, including work on himself.

This pregnancy ended in a miscarriage. My brain went back in forth between God protecting me from what I can't see and God punishing me for the past abortions. Truth be told, I didn't want to have his baby, only because of how he treated me when I found out. Those were the actions that showed me who he really was as a man.   H e wasn't the accountable man that I imagined would raise my children. I was really firm in my beliefs that I was not having another abortion. I felt like I had learned my lesson. I was actually on birth control this time. Since God makes no mistakes, I said if it is meant to be, it will work out for my good; if not, God won't let it be. So I want to believe that the miscarriage was God's protection and that I will be able to have kids in the future.

The relationship with this last man is what made me learn the most grace. I realized I couldn't be mad that he didn't fit into the plan that God had for me, which brought me back to the relationship with you again. You brought me as far as you could, and God has been doing the rest. That's the only thing that made me feel inclined to reach out to you after you ignored me for over a year.

Chapter six
FORGIVING YOU

F orgiving you was no easy task. Ultimately it took me to look in the mirror at myself to forgive you. It took me to realize that we all make mistakes, some worse than others. Everything I just told you in this letter was not even close to describing the pain I endured. I left out some details. My life has been a never-ending roller coaster. For the longest time, I blamed those pains on you. I blamed you for not loving me or showing me what real love looks like. I blamed you for being bullied in school because I didn't look or act like everyone else. I blamed you for my love life resembling a soap opera.

I'm sure you could tell how angry I was by the first message that I sent you. It had been almost three years since I had last spoken to you. Not only was I upset that you didn't reach out, I was agonized that you were able to live your life as if nothing had happened. I was tired of holding it in and not confronting you.

Out of anger, I texted you late at night on January 30, 2020:

"I cannot stand you. Everything that you put me through as a kid, and you own up to none of it. You never even apologized. You act as though nothing ever happened, yet I

have to live a life full of trauma and wonder why I act the way I act, and it's all because of you. You decided to make poor decisions. You decided to do drugs and do them right in front of us. There is no fucking reason I should have known how to smoke heroin as a little girl and picking up stuff off of the floor mimicking you. There is no reason that you should have thought it was ever okay for him to touch me when I WAS ONLY 5 YEARS FUCKING OLD. God forbid you are allowing that creep shit to happen to my little sisters. There is no reason that anyone should have been having sex with me like that. And every single time, you lead me right into that room. I'll never forget the fucking day that you said it's gone be okay. He just wants to lick you. All of this so you can get high. And I'll never live a fucking normal life. Ever. You robbed me of every piece of childhood or innocence I would ever have. Bouncing back and forth from house to house and school to school. Now all of a sudden, you're supposed to be mother of the fucking year to liyah and keke, yea fucking right. You can't be there for nobody but your fucking self. All you think about is your fucking self. You are selfish. I am sick of pretending like everything's okay. That's why I can't talk to you and why I damn sure don't want to see you. You are no mother to me. I don't even know how you sleep at night. Look in the fucking mirror."

The first year that you didn't text me back, I was on an emotional roller coaster. The pandemic had just started, so I had all of the time in the world to think. Think about you, the heartache, the disappointments, the setbacks, the shame, the guilt, the burdens, and all of the storms. When I sent you that message, I wanted you to feel that. I needed you to see the storm cloud that I was running from. I needed you to see beyond everything that I've accomplished and focus on what it took to get there for a second.

Why do people do that? Why do people see all of the things that you are accomplishing and assume life is good? Most of the family see me as standoffish or stuck up. I only seem standoffish because I don't fit in when I'm around. All of my cousins' struggles were nowhere near the things I've witnessed or experienced. Everything that I went through made me different. Pain made me different. I only seem stuck up because they only see the products I produce but not the war that existed inside of me.

I don't know if you have ever been at war with yourself, but it's almost like having multiple personalities. All of your personalities have different beliefs. So you may hear one voice saying how good you look, another one that points out your stretch marks, and another one saying that insecurity is why we got hurt. It's a battle of the thoughts, and may the loudest one win.

Imagine having so many obnoxiously loud thoughts telling you everything that you're not. Now imagine deciphering which thoughts should be there and making them louder, and dispose of the rest. I realized trying to ignore them doesn't work because they can always get louder. Talking back was the only way to end the war down on the inside of me.

At first, I thought talking back and cursing you out in a text message was the same. When I first texted you, I felt a little relief until you never texted back. Being ignored reminded me of why I never spoke up in the first place. I already felt ignored by you for so long. I knew this time was different, though. I knew that you ignoring me had way more to do with yourself than me.

Since I had already been on this journey of putting myself in your shoes, I did the same thing when I thought about the message. The truth is, I knew why you didn't respond. You felt attacked. There was so much animosity. I threw the very things that were keeping you stuck in your face. Since we've been acting like it never happened for so long, I'm sure it was a reality check.

If I hurt you by sending that message, it was not my intention; I just tried to get some attention. I just needed you to know that the weight of the burden was keeping my feet planted. Trying to get attention to my pain awakened me to yours. It made me see that you couldn't be there for me because you were barely holding yourself up. I know what type of weight you're carrying. If no one else has, I give you the permission to put the weight down. I forgive you because you're just like me, and I'm just like you.

Coming to this realization, having grace, and needing to really forgive you led me to text you again. On September 12, 2021, I sent:

"Hey, I'm not sure why you ignored my message to you, but it's been over a year. Maybe I was too aggressive, but I had to say how I felt. I feel like, as an adult, I want you to talk to me. I don't want to hate you, I want to understand you and the decisions you made because they also affected me. I know that no one is perfect; I know we all make bad decisions whether you are a parent or not. I know it's also probably hard for you to talk about because maybe you regret those decisions but could you at least say that to me? I've grown to be very understanding and forgiving, and I forgive you because I no longer can carry any hate in my heart. I can no longer keep dwelling on past things. I try to think of good memories with you, and we have a lot. Remember how we used to watch all the cartoons together? Your favorite was courage, the cowardly dog. And how

we would watch all the movies together, and your favorite was the predators and mines was jaws. We used to watch charmed and the superman show, and remember how you loved law and order. Do you remember how we all used to play spades and I was always on your team and we would win, or playing monopoly with us. You didn't do everything all bad. You tried your best with what you knew. You did what you had to do to make sure we had some kind of home, were fed and had clothes and shoes. I want to rebuild a relationship with you. I hope all is well, and I hope you can respond to me this time."

When you responded, I cried. I didn't know how much I needed to forgive you and hear from you until I did. You said, "I'm sorry for everything; I truly hope all is well with you. I'm paying for my past. I am just struggling and trying to survive. I miss you so much. I hear you are doing well for yourself. I've come a long way also, one year clean." Then when you asked me for money a week later, I thought we'd never have a relationship. The truth is, I pray for your peace more than I pray for a relationship with you.

The biggest thing that transformed my life after God was self-love. I stopped trying to be good enough for everybody. I realized I was more than enough and started deciding who was good enough for me. After experiencing so much trauma, you think that you are damaged goods. That's what the enemy wants you to believe. He wants you to believe that God can't make a way out of no way. There is nothing you can't do, Mama. That dream that you had before the calamity can still be accomplished. The roadblocks you had along the way can be removed; you just have to have enough faith to see past them.

While we may or may not ever have a relationship, I'm still rooting for you. I still love you. I forgive you for everything. I understand you, and I see you. You are so resilient. You are deserving of all the things your heart desires. All those times I wanted to give up in this past year, I thought of you. I reflected on how much weight you were carrying but never threw in the tile. The fact that you are still surviving should let you know that there is a blessing with your name on it. Be proud of yourself for pushing through and not letting the thoughts consume you. Be proud of the woman that has come from you because I will break every shackle. Also, go find yourself. Every relationship, pregnancy, and hardship took a piece of you. Go put you back together with nothing but the pieces that create a phenomenal woman.

Thank you for never giving up. I know your best wasn't the best, but thank you for trying. Thank you for bringing me into this world.

I pray that you find the blessing that God has prepared for you. I pray you get tired of your own stuff. I pray God places someone in your life that gets you to release the self-limiting beliefs that you have. I pray that you heal those things down on the inside of you. I pray you dig so deep until you hit the mine inside of you. I pray that you learn the power of self-love. I pray that my siblings learn the power of self-love. I pray that you start searching for a bigger meaning. I pray that you recognize your strength. I pray that God comes and hugs you so tight that depression has no choice but to let you go. I pray you start seeing that you deserve so much more. I pray you have a revelation of how worthy you are no matter what decisions you have made. No matter what you have done or been through. I pray you experience real love with a man that never disrespects you or enables bad traits in you. I pray that generational curse up off of you. I pray that addiction up off of you. I pray you tap into your superpower. I know you didn't experience the love you needed, but God says he will give it to you. I know you might feel like it is too late, but God says you're right on time. We serve an on-time kind of God, Mama. We serve a god that doesn't mind starting over. We serve a God that will direct your steps. A forgiving, miracle-working, way-making God. You are a descendant of royalty, and I pray you start walking like it, talking like it, and loving like it.

With Love,

Tho